Doth Geister

UTAH SKIING

A
SCENIC VIEW

JOHN GEISTER

To To my children, Megan and J.R. with
loving anticipation of skiing together.
With deep appreciation to my mother, Toi.

Published by John Geister Publishing LLC.
471 Heritage Park Boulevard, Suite 5
Layton, Utah 84041

Printed in the U.S. by Precision Litho
2305 South 1070 West
Salt Lake City, Utah 84119

ISBN 0-9706280-0-5

Ordering books or Photographs

To order more copies of *Utah Skiing*, posters, or fine art prints
of any photograph in *Utah Skiing*, go to our web site,
utahskiing.ws

Photographers Comments

I have been a dedicated skier for well over thirty years and have enjoyed the sport for many reasons: the thrill of going fast, the exhilaration of skiing the steep and deep, the serenity of floating in bottomless powder and the camaraderie of being with other free spirited skiers. But underlying all of these feelings is my love for the mountains.

Every resort I have ever skied has several places where I would just have to stop and soak in the beauty. Many times this year I would be setting up for a photo and a group of four or five skiers would come up and stop in total silence. After about a minute some one would boldly say "wow that's incredible." I found myself using that word "incredible" a lot when describing my ski days.

I'm at peace in the mountains. I feel safe, as if I were an infant in my mother's arms. For me it is almost a religious experience. I feel closer to God.

One day I was standing on a ridge top (over eleven thousand feet) in sixty mile an hour winds with the temperature at five degrees, the wind chill would be about fifty five below zero, I was involved in taking pictures of some awesome views and I didn't even notice the bitter conditions. Instead I was thinking "what a great day to be alive!" On those crystal clear days, well you just can't beat it.

I do hope these pictures give you a small appreciation for my mountains, and for those of you that have never experienced the mountains of Utah I invite you to ski Utah and enjoy the scenic views.

John Geister

Contents

P.O. Box 8007
Alta, Utah 84092
(801) 359-1078
www.alta.com

P.O. Box 190008
Brian Head, Utah 84719
(435) 677-2035
www.brianhead.com
E-mail: info@brianhead.com

28

Star Route
Brighton, Utah 84121
(801) 532-4731 (800) 873-5512
www.skibrighton.com

4000 The Canyons Resort Drive
Park City, Utah 84090
(435) 649-5400

DEER VALLEY RESORT

P.O. Box 1525
Park City, Utah 84060
(435) 649-1000 (800) 424-DEER
www.deervalley.com

P.O. Box 511
Beaver, Utah 84713
(435) 438-5433 (888) 881-7669 (SNOW)
www.elkmeadows.com

P.O. Box 39
Park City, Utah 84060
(800) 222-7275
www.parkcitymountain.com

P.O. Box 450
Eden, Utah 84310
(801) 745-3772
Snow Line: (801) 745-3771
www.powdermountain.com
E-mail: powdermountain@powdermountain.com

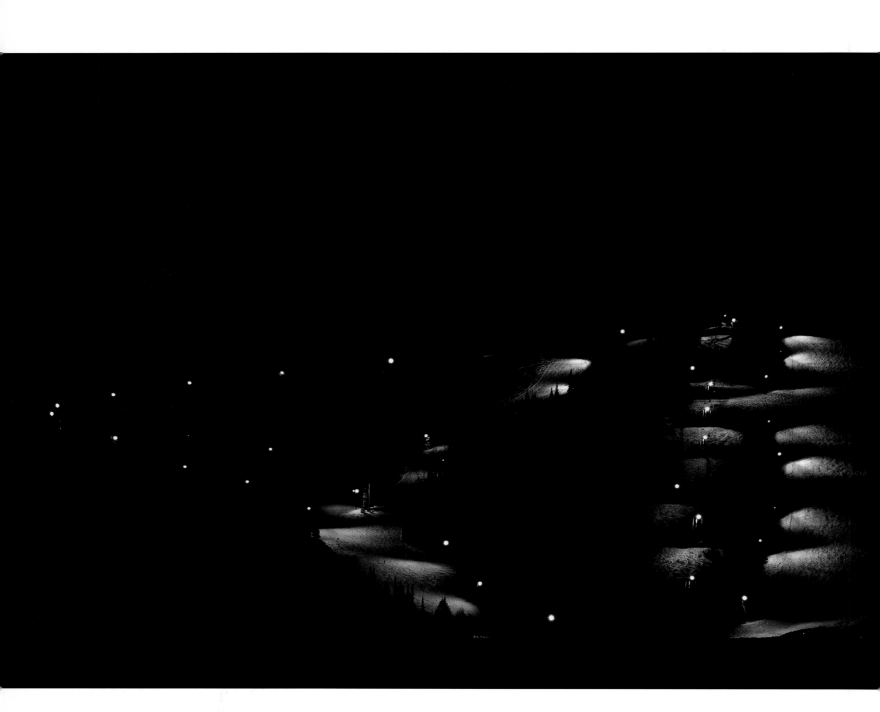

3925 Snowbasin Road
Huntsville, Utah 84317
(801) 399-1135
(888) 437-5488
www.snowbasin.com

snowbird.

Little Cottonwood Canyon HWY 210
Snowbird, Utah 84092
Resort Information: (801) 742-2222
Reservations: (800) 640-2002
www.snowbird.com

12000 Big Cottonwood Canyon
Solitude, Utah 84121
(801) 534-1400
(800) 748-4754
www.skisolitude.com

sundance

RR-3, Box A-1
Sundance, Utah 84604
(801) 225-4107 (800) 892-1600
www.sundance-utah.com

Special Thanks to

Connie Marshall / Alta

Craig McCarthy
Clark Krause / Brianhead

Dan Malstrom / Brighton

Katie Eldridge
Carrie Meater / The Canyons

Christa Graff / Deer Valley

Jim Collins
Gene Gatza / Elk Meadows

Michelle Palmer
Melissa O'Brien / Park City

Carolyn & Lavar Lowther
Mark Poulsen / Powder Mountain

Gray Reynolds
Kent Matthews / Snow Basin

Larry Jackstien
Fred Rollins / Snowbird

Dave DeSeelhorst
Nikki Brush / Solitude

Mark Preiss
Laurie Bott / Sundance

Richard B. Glasmann

Margie & Dick Shanklin